TALE OF A FISH

Quran Stories for Little Hearts

by

S Khan

Goodwordkidz

Helping you build a family of faith

A very old and powerful community used to live around 800 B.C., in Nineveh, an ancient town believed to have been on the left bank of the Tigris river, some 230 miles north-west of Baghdad. Allah sent the Prophet Yunus (Jonah) عَلَيْهِ السَّلَام to this community to guide them on to the right path.

3

4

Yunus ﷺ did as Allah said and went to these people. He gave them His message and warned them to turn away from their wickedness. Yunus ﷺ preached to them for a long time, but they paid no heed to his words. When he realized that they intended to continue on the wrong path, he warned them about how bad their actions were and that in the end they might be made to suffer. Angry and despairing, Yunus ﷺ left these people.

5

Yunus علیہ السلام moved out of the city and headed towards the seaport where there were ships tied up, waiting to sail. One, Yunus علیہ السلام found, was due to sail to a far off land. He boarded the ship.

6

As soon as it was out at sea, the sky grew dark, and there was a terrible storm. The fierce wind began to whip the water up into huge waves which crashed against the hull of the ship.

As the storm grew worse, the waves became like towering walls of water which came crashing down on the ship's deck. The sailors worked with all their strength to try to keep the ship on course.

They even threw some of the cargo overboard, to make the ship easier to control. But the ship's strong timber seemed as thin as matchwood in the teeth of the storm. Soon, they knew, it would break up and they would all drown.

Thinking their ill-luck was due to some slave having run away from his master, they drew lots to find the run-away and hurl him overboard. The name of Yunus  was picked out in the draw. So he was forced to jump from the ship.

As he struggled in the water, gasping for breath, a great whale appeared out of the depths of the sea and swallowed him up. (The fish that swallowed Yunus ﷺ may have been a sperm whale. Such whales are known to visit the eastern Mediterranean sea. With their large throats, they can swallow the body of a man whole).

Suddenly Yunus ﷺ found himself in the dark, damp insides of the huge fish. He had not drowned. He was still alive! Now Yunus ﷺ realized that he had left the people of Nineveh too early without completing the task assigned by Allah. As a rule, once it became clear that a nation had rejected Allah's message, the prophet who had been the bearer of that message was commanded by Allah to leave—but only if he had done his very best to reform his hearers. Then Allah punished the erring people as a mark of His wrath. But Yunus ﷺ had not waited for Allah's order. He had simply gone away, leaving the people of Nineveh to their doom.

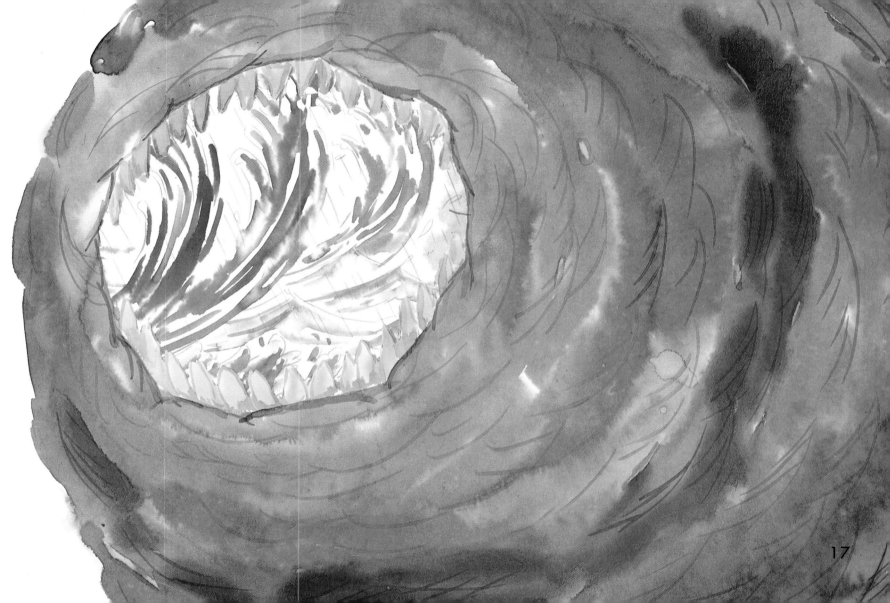

When Yunus ﷺ realized his mistake, he cried from the depth of darkness: "There is no god but You. Glory be to You! I have done wrong." Allah heard his prayers. The Quran says that if he had not said he was sorry and glorified Allah in his prayers, he would have stayed in the belly of the fish till the Day of Judgement.

The fish, by the command of Allah, swam close to the land and brought Yunus علیه السلام safely on to the beach, where he found himself under a tree called Yaqtin (gourd-tree). It shaded him from the heat of the sun while he recovered from his ordeal. It also gave him a delicious fruit full of juice to quench his thirst.

Yunus  then returned to his people and preached to them again. All of them, over one hundred thousand, responded to his call.

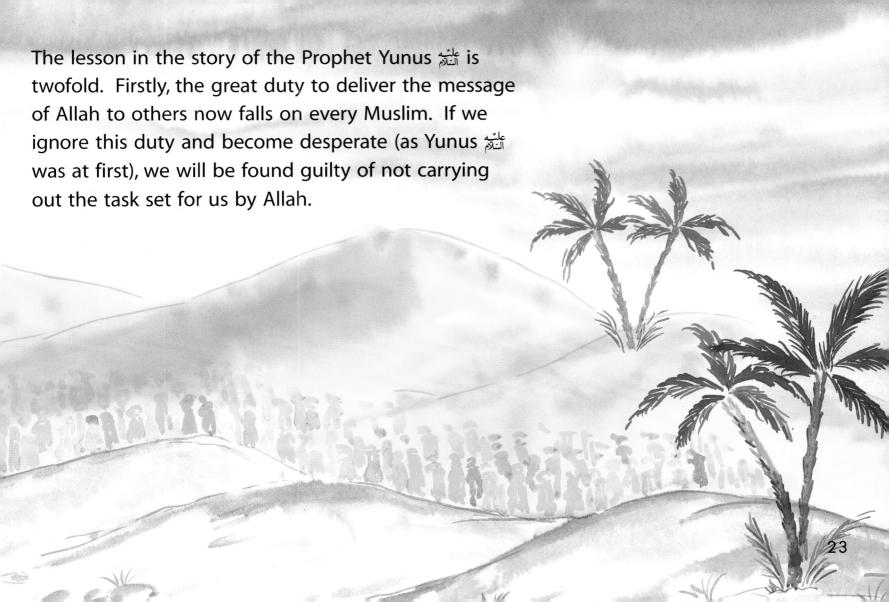

The lesson in the story of the Prophet Yunus ﷺ is twofold. Firstly, the great duty to deliver the message of Allah to others now falls on every Muslim. If we ignore this duty and become desperate (as Yunus ﷺ was at first), we will be found guilty of not carrying out the task set for us by Allah.

23

Secondly, the courage which was shown by Yunus عليه السلام as he nearly drowned is a great example and shows us that we should never despair of the mercy of Allah. If we are on the right path and say we are sorry for our failings, Allah will help us as miraculously as He did when Yunus عليه السلام was saved from the raging sea by the giant fish.

Find Out More
To know more about the message and meaning of Allah's words, look up the following parts of the Quran which tell the story of the Prophet Yunus عليه السلام:

Surah al-Anbiya 21:87-88
Surah as-Saffat 37:139-148

عليه السلام *Alayhis Salam* 'May peace be upon him.'
The customary blessing on the prophets.